ASTRAL PROJECTION

Learn How to Travel the Astral Plane and Explore Lucid Dreaming

(Proven Methods and Techniques of Traveling the Astral Plane With Obe Out-of-body Experience)

Donna Koehler

Published by Tomas Edwards

© **Donna Koehler**

All Rights Reserved

Astral Projection: Learn How to Travel the Astral Plane and Explore Lucid Dreaming (Proven Methods and Techniques of Traveling the Astral Plane With Obe Out-of-body Experience)

ISBN 978-1-989744-80-2

All rights reserved. No part of this guide may be reproduced in any form without permission in writing from the publisher except in the case of brief quotations embodied in critical articles or reviews.

Legal & Disclaimer

The information contained in this book is not designed to replace or take the place of any form of medicine or professional medical advice. The information in this book has been provided for educational and entertainment purposes only.

The information contained in this book has been compiled from sources deemed reliable, and it is accurate to the best of the Author's knowledge; however, the Author cannot guarantee its accuracy and validity and cannot be held liable for any errors or omissions. Changes are periodically made to this book. You must consult your doctor or get professional medical advice before using any of the suggested remedies, techniques, or information in this book.

Upon using the information contained in this book, you agree to hold harmless the Author from and against any damages, costs, and expenses, including any legal fees potentially resulting from the application of any of the information provided by this guide. This disclaimer applies to any damages or injury caused by the use and application, whether directly or indirectly, of any advice or information presented, whether for breach of contract, tort, negligence, personal injury, criminal intent, or under any other cause of action.

You agree to accept all risks of using the information presented inside this book. You need to consult a professional medical practitioner in order to ensure you are both able and healthy enough to participate in this program.

Table of Contents

INTRODUCTION 1

CHAPTER 1: WHAT IS ASTRAL PROJECTION? 5

CHAPTER 2: BENEFITS OF ASTRAL PROJECTION 20

CHAPTER 3: THE ASTRAL PLANES 28

CHAPTER 4: HOW TO PERFORM ASTRAL PROJECTION 32

CHAPTER 5: PREPARING FOR ASTRAL PROJECTION 42

CHAPTER 6: HOW TO EXPERIENCE ASTRAL PROJECTION AND NEVER BE THE SAME AGAIN 51

CHAPTER 7: PREPARING FOR ASTRAL PROJECTION AND TRAVEL 57

CHAPTER 8: DIFFERENT WAYS TO ASTRAL TRAVEL 71

CHAPTER 9: YOUR FIRST ASTRAL PROJECTION 86

CHAPTER 10: MEDITATION AND HYPNOSIS 93

CHAPTER 11: TECHNIQUES 111

CHAPTER 12: SEPARATING THE ASTRAL SELF FROM THE PHYSICAL BODY 117

CHAPTER 13: REMOTE VIEWING 123

CONCLUSION... 133

Introduction

Among the out of body experiences people may have, probably the most intriguing is Astral Projection. To understand this phenomenon though, it is important to first understand what exactly an out of body experience is.

Out of body experience or OBE is an experience that involves you feeling like you're floating out of your own body. Sometimes people who have OBEs can see their own bodies, or they see the situations they are in from a different perspective outside their bodies. This view is more commonly referred to as an autoscopic experience.

Types of Out of Body Experiences

There are many types of OBEs, and they can be triggered in many different ways such as brain trauma, near death experiences (NDEs), use of psychedelic drugs like LSD, sleep and sensory deprivation or overload. Though there has been a heated debate on the subject in recent years, most scientists agree that OBEs are dissociative experiences caused by psychological and neurological factors such as schizophrenia or brain damage.

OBEs are usually placed into two categories depending on how they were achieved. The categories are induced and spontaneous OBEs. Spontaneous OBEs are unplanned and often occur as a result of extreme stress, anxiety, severe physical trauma or extreme physical exertion. They may occur during sleep, usually just before or just after a person has finally fallen asleep.

Spontaneous OBEs caused by extreme physical exertion can result in what is sometimes called a bilocal state. This state is sometimes experienced by high-altitude climbers and marathon runners. In such cases, the affected person can see themselves from a different perspective (autoscopically), and they can feel and perceive everything that their body is doing and going through. This makes it seem like both the autoscopic and ordinary perceptions are happening simultaneously.

Induced out of body experiences are, planned and deliberately carried out by the individual. They can be induced chemically by using hallucinogenic drugs like Ketamine, Tenamphetamine (MDA) and LSD.

They can also be induced mechanically in a host of different ways, many of them involving direct stimulation of the brain. Procedures such as magnetic stimulation, direct stimulation of the vestibular cortex (the area of the brain that deals with movement and balance), and electronic stimulation of the temporoparietal junction (an area of the brain that deals with cognitive functions) have all been used to induce OBEs.

Sensory deprivation and conversely, sensory overload have also been used to induce an OBE. However, the best way to induce an OBE is to do so mentally. Mental induction usually involves falling asleep without losing awareness (commonly known as lucid dreaming) or going into a deep trance using meditation and visualisation techniques.

Chapter 1: What Is Astral Projection?

"Astral projection" seems to mean many different things to different people. Various cultures over the centuries have had their own interpretations of what astral projection is, who can engage in it, and how they initiate an experience. Modern practitioners often integrate various cultural techniques and wisdom into their own practice, making the most of the wide range of information that is now available.

With all the different models of reality and techniques presented by different cultures, there doesn't seem to be any wrong way to astral project. That being said, there are certainly best practices and some very important areas that one must diligently cover in one's own practice, regardless of which philosophies are integrated. For instance, setting clear intentions, establishing boundaries, setting up protection, and meditation are all crucial elements of a safe and productive astral projection practice. We'll go into more depth on these subjects in later chapters.

For all the intercultural differences, every astral philosophy seems to agree that astral projection is a form of travel conducted by an energetic body that exists beyond the limitations of the physical body. Overall, it is believed that every person has an energetic body that serves as an intermediary between the physical body and the soul. The soul is the animating force inside of the physical body, like the hand inside of the glove. The energetic body is yet another layer of what makes up a person, another piece of one's consciousness.

Because the energetic body is not the soul itself, it is free to move about outside of the body without causing a person to die. These "out of body" experiences are very similar to what people describe during near-death experiences, the major difference being that astral projection is performed consciously and deliberately, while near-death experiences happen spontaneously, when one is close to death or experiencing a deep trauma. Near-death experiences may even involve the soul's departure from the body, especially in cases where one physically dies for a few minutes and is then brought back by doctors or paramedics. Without the scientific means to measure such phenomena, however, it is hard to say for certain.

It is commonly believed that the energetic body is connected to the physical body through a silver "cord," which is made up of the soul's own energy. This cord is extremely difficult to cut, and it never gets lost or "tangled." The silver cord acts as a guide back to the body so that no matter how far the energetic or astral body travels, it can always return home.

Some believe that during an experience of astral projection, the energetic body never truly leaves the physical body at all, but that all the processes happen internally. In this philosophy, astral projection can be understood as a metaphor for developing psychic abilities, so that practitioners "see" through their third eye and access information they could not otherwise know. Still others believe that an astral projection experience is actually the individual's way of accessing the deep unconscious mind, which is connected to the collective unconscious and can thus retrieve information that is already available to everyone on the unconscious level. While everyone must ultimately decide what seems true for him- or herself, this book will deal with astral projection as an out of body spiritual experience.

What is the astral realm?

Just as people have different interpretations of what astral projection is, so do they have different beliefs about the astral realm. The short answer is that the astral realm is the "place" your energetic body or consciousness travels to during astral projection. Is this a true location or world that takes up physical space in the universe? It depends on where you go, but generally, the answer is no.

The astral realm is an energetic realm that exists alongside the physical one. Only the third dimension, the one we inhabit, takes up physical space in the sense that we know it, while many believe that the other dimensions are home to spiritual and energetic realms of higher and higher frequency. We'll get more into frequency in later chapters.

Western esoteric tradition distinguishes between the astral realm and the etheric realm. In this philosophy, the etheric realm is basically synonymous with the "mundane" world of physical reality that we function in every day. The etheric realm, being the energetic aspect of the world of the physical, is still bound by the laws of time and space. However, time and space are more fluid in the etheric realm, and the two realms of the etheric and physical interact in interesting ways. While they exist side by side, they tend to function on their own channels, affected by one another yet most often being experienced independently of one another by the beings who inhabit them.

Every once in a while, a being from one realm will stray into the other realm. For instance, an intersection such as this is responsible for ghost sightings, when a being inhabiting the etheric realm suddenly appears in the world of the physical. For this reason, many believe that the etheric realm is one and the same as the spirit world.

The astral realm, on the other hand, is not bound to the physical world in any way that we know. Time doesn't seem to exist here, or if it does, it follows radically different laws than the ones we are used to. The astral realm is a world of infinite possibilities, where people can journey to fantastic realities inhabited by otherworldly beings.

Many say that people traveling in the astral realm have the ability to access the Akashic records, an infinite energetic library that stores all knowledge, emotions, thoughts, events, and possibilities of past, present, and future for every living and energetic being across every world and dimension. Sounds pretty epic, does it not?

Whereas the etheric realm is as literal to interpretation as the physical world, the astral realm is a place of symbol and mystery. People often come here to gain important insights for their personal journeys, either through working with the Akashic records or receiving guidance from some of the benevolent beings who inhabit these energetic worlds. Of course, not all beings who hang around the astral world are benevolent, but we'll go more into this in later chapters.

Due to the dreamlike quality of the astral realm, some claim that it is indeed the place our consciousness travels to when we dream. While some believe that dreaming is a form of astral projection, others take this to mean that the experience of astral projection is simply a form of lucid dreaming and that the astral realm is no more than the realm of the unconscious. This view is not meant to diminish the wonder and the very powerful work that can stem from conscious exploration of the unconscious, but simply to help put it into a context that those with a more scientific disposition can understand. People are free to believe what they want; the important thing is that those who need the healing and guidance find a way to access it, whatever the mechanism behind the phenomenon.

Different Cultural Interpretations

Understanding how different cultures interpret astral projection can help you find the techniques that work best for you.

Whether their beliefs help you with your own understanding, or they provide you with a structured pathway for accessing these realms for yourself, knowing as much as you can on the subject will prove to be of huge benefit.

Ancient Egypt

Ancient Egyptians held a philosophy of energetic experience outside of the physical body very similar to astral projection. In their beliefs, the soul (ba) was capable of traveling outside of the body through the "subtle body" (ka). The similarity between the two words hints at the link between the soul and the subtle body, much like the link between the soul and the energetic or astral body in the philosophy of astral projection.

Ancient China

The ancient Taoist alchemical practice of China instructs practitioners on the creation of the energetic body. In this philosophy, the astral body is created through the use of breathing meditations, in which the traveler envisions his own energy into a "pearl," which then circulates as it begins to take form.

India

In Indian tradition, astral projection is a Siddhi, a supernatural or spiritual power or ability that can be attained through the practice of sadhanas like yoga and meditation. Famous Indian spiritual figures attest to the reality of astral projection. The famous guru Paramahansa Yogananda claims to have witnessed a feat of astral projection when a prominent swami used the method to perform a miracle. Osho, the great teacher, says that he himself is a practitioner of astral projection.

Japan

In Japan, the energetic body is known as the ikiryo, and it is believed to be a sort of soul that exists outside of and independent of the physical body. Some ikiryo manifest before a person who has wronged the sender to curse or haunt them. One would need to hold a particularly strong grudge before an ikiryo would have the power to go forth in that way. Benevolent ikiryo, on the other hand, can manifest when a person is extremely ill or in a coma. These energetic bodies can serve to communicate on behalf of the individual, or they can simply allow a part of the person to move around when otherwise bedridden.

Native Americans

Different Native American tribes of North and South America have their own specific mythology and terminology surrounding the concept of astral projection. However, the common thread is that in most traditions, shamans of the tribe can use astral projection, or spirit journeying, to perform important spiritual work. The uses of shamanic journeying vary greatly, but some common practices include journeying to receive healing instructions from plant teachers, seeking the meanings of omens and performing divination, assisting warriors in battle or on a hunt, and consulting with spirits for advice.

There is much, much more to learn on the subjects of astral projection in different cultures. If this is an area of study that interests you, you should definitely consider doing more research to continue learning and deepening your understanding.

Is it safe?

Every responsible prospective astral traveler will inevitably ask this very question, and indeed, it is a monumentally important one to ask. Generally, very few of us have extensive experience with the energetic realms within our current lifetimes, and these powerful worlds and the beings that inhabit them are certainly no matter to be taken lightly.

Many practitioners and advocates of astral projection insist that this is a completely safe, no-risk practice. The silver cord will always bring you back to your body, so there is no need to fear getting lost or becoming stuck outside of your body. These same people will tell you that there is no risk of harm from entities that you will encounter in the energetic realms, for only benevolent beings reside in these realms. Others will acknowledge that not all beings have your best interests in mind, but that you can avoid encounters with mischievous or malevolent beings simply through setting your intention.

Some spiritual practitioners caution that malevolent beings can cause harm to your energetic body, either through using energetic "weapons" or bringing about a traumatic psychic experience. There are even those who caution that some of these entities can enter your physical body while your energetic body is away, having left a vacancy that they can occupy.

These warnings are not to completely dissuade you from pursuing the astral projection experience, but merely to help you understand that this endeavor is not one to rush into without training, preparation, and careful consideration. While some will steadfastly insist that there is no such danger, it would be ultimately irresponsible for a resource not to warn and prepare you for anything that might come up. For instance, even without the worry of harmful beings, a traumatic experience in the energetic realm can affect you just as deeply as one in the physical world can, so it's important to make sure that you are psychologically prepared for whatever you may see and feel.

Most of these issues can be prevented or addressed with careful precautionary measures. Practicing astral projection safely and successfully requires a lot of training and preparation, and one should never skip these steps in their enthusiasm to get started.

The spiritual worlds one can access through astral projection, however, are certainly wondrous and fantastic, and it is easy to see why so many people are excited to explore these realms for themselves. The work that one can do through astral projection and the knowledge and healing that can be accessed are certainly wonderful payoffs that are well worth the wait. Take your time, do your due diligence, and enjoy the experience when the time is right.

Chapter 2: Benefits Of Astral Projection

The concept of astral projection can be intimidating to some. It sounds like a far-fetched idea to those who aren't used to such spiritual concepts. The fact of the matter is though that astral projection is something that is very possible for anyone to do.

It just takes the right attitude and willingness to do the techniques. But why would a person want to use astral projection? Is there a benefit outside of experience something most do not typically? The answer is a simple yes.

There are many great benefits for using astral projection to explore other planes of existence. These benefits will become apparent to those who try out astral projection for themselves, but we will list and speak on the most common benefits.

It can help you to decide whether undertaking an astral journey is something you will be interested in doing. After reading through the benefits, you will be completely ready to want to become a traveler of the astral plane.

One of the most easily understood benefits of astral projection is that of relieving stress. When you find yourself travelling on the astral plane, you will feel a great sense of inner peace. It is a happy experience to be able to unchain yourself from your physical body and explore new realms.

Doing so will help you to relieve the stress of your day in many ways. It is an escape from your physical reality. It is the physical world that is bringing all of the stress into your mind and spirit.

Everything from obligations to family to a hectic work schedule can drag a person down and make them feel like there is no escape. Astral projection can become that escape for you.

If you get into the habit of practicing astral projection nightly or even just once or twice a week it can feel like a vacation from your everyday life. Use this to your advantage to relief your stress often and give yourself a well-deserved break.

Self-discovery is another great thing that can be gleaned from your time with astral projection. People don't always realize that we are more than our physical selves. We are not just a collection of meat and bones given intelligence.

We are a consciousness that is capable of so many different things. Exploring the astral plane can help a person to realize that there is more to life than just the physical.

Journeying like this can give you a great boost to your self-confidence because you realize that you are more than just what people see you as. You are a person who is capable of making great discoveries, both about yourself and the world around you. Astral projection will aid you towards that end.

The ability to see things from a different perspective is an astounding thing. When you only look at things from one way, you can find yourself possessing a jaded perspective. Astral projection allows you to see things in a light that is beyond the physical.

Looking at the problems present in your life from this new perspective can help you to solve some of your greatest dilemmas. Focusing on that which troubles you during your time in your astral body can lead you to conclusions you may not have considered otherwise.

It is a worthwhile endeavor to look to yourself for guidance during your astral journey. You can also seek wisdom on the astral plane itself, perhaps discovering something new that can shed a different light on a situation in your physical life.

Those looking to develop their spirituality are in for a treat when beginning to explore with astral projection. You will find that you are more in tune with your spiritual self the more you delve into the astral realm. Faith is not an easy thing for some people, but when you have something tangible to explore it can make the difference for those not possessing great faith.

Understanding that there is a spiritual world out there to explore will increase your belief in many core spiritual concepts. The after-life for example seems so much more feasible when you regularly experience other planes of existence.

It is easier to think that your consciousness could continue outside of your physical body when it dies, when you are regularly exploring without being tethered to that physical body. Your spiritual side will grow by leaps and bounds as you begin to understand that which is beyond the physical.

Other benefits people have experienced from using astral projection are increased healing capabilities, a nurturing of psychic capabilities and increased mind power. Sometimes when your body is in need of healing, the conscious mind can hinder the healing process.

When you spend time in the astral plane, people say that their bodies heal quicker when their consciousness is removed from their body. This can be a great benefit and will allow you to bring greater health into your life.

The nurturing of psychic abilities has also been reported by those who practice astral projection. Psychic abilities such as clairvoyance and developing one's third eye can more easily grow when you practice astral projection.

It helps you to tap into your spirit, and the power of your mind that normally lies dormant. Having a sense of things that are going to come is certainly a great power that many would appreciate having at their disposal.

This isn't as far-fetched as some might be thinking, as many people throughout history have showcased an ability to predict events or understand that which is to come with a greater clarity than most. Increasing your mind power is something that will happen through astral projection as well.

When travelling to these different planes you will be using areas of your conscious mind that you never knew existed. Areas of the brain that were once dormant will be utilized regularly during your astral experiences. Your sense of creativity and the power of your imagination will increase greatly due to this new form of stimuli as well.

Now that you understand the benefits of astral projection you probably want to know how you can begin this journey yourself. As mentioned before, meditation and lucid dreaming are the two accessible portals into the astral plane.

Just knowing that may not be enough to make the jump into becoming a traveler of the astral plane. Because of this we are going to highlight techniques that can be used for the beginner to start his or her journey. These techniques are very easy to understand, and through reading about this you will be aided in your desire to tap into this new experience.

Chapter 3: The Astral Planes

Astral Projection involves moving through the Astral Planes. You can encounter other spirits, learn from them, and travel to faraway places. It is helpful if you have been to a place before, so you can more easily visualize the situation. So, what is this Astral Plane that everyone in the mysticism fields speaks of?

The plane is where souls go after they die to work on karmic issues. If a spirit is required to do so, it will return to Earth in an act of reincarnation. In Buddhism, the soul gathers karma and can either move up in the worlds or down, and as the spirit gains more positive karma, it moves into higher worlds. These worlds are the astral planes, and they can be accessed by the living, too. Your ability to travel up through the higher worlds is based on your vibrations. If you have enough positive vibration, you can move to higher worlds, or spheres. This is also a helpful protection technique if you happen to be pursued by a negative energy. See the chapter on protection for more information about this.

The various levels can be mapped to different types of beings. The lowest is not a place you want your soul to stay. It is here that souls are almost trapped, for they cannot move on to higher planes but they also do not have a body to return to in the physical world. They have physical desires just like we do, but they do not have bodies so they cannot satisfy them. This is hellish level. The next level is more pleasant, because the souls there are able to build their own worlds – very similar to lucid dreaming but in a different dimension. The spirits here often find friends and family among them, but the ultimate goal is to rise through all the planes after death. You may visit here, too, if you wish. The next plane in line is more mental, and the spirits here are attempting to work out their intellectual pursuits before moving higher – as you can image, this puts mental desires about physical in the astral world. The levels then move up in progressively more spiritual aspects until the final realm is reached. In Buddhism, the goal is to attain ever higher levels of spirituality until the soul is in a state that requires no more reincarnation, as the karmic deeds performed before affording the soul a very long, contemplative, and content life in a very high plane. The beings on these high astral planes are similar to gods, for they live for eons in their current form.

Now, you may want to stay on some of the lower levels that are more closely connected to Earth. You need not fear the lower realms, even if there are spirits there that cannot move on. You may even move your soul around to visit places on earth, if you would like. This is a major goal of many astral projectors: they want to see other parts of the world now or in a past time. Some people might use this to protect their loved ones or simply to broaden their experiences when they cannot physically go somewhere due to lack of money or otherwise. But what if you wanted to expand your knowledge? Is there a way to find access a library of some sort that contains all the knowledge of the world? I do not mean the Internet, either. This library is known as the Akashic Record. Let's see how the Akashic Record can first be accessed and then what can be learned from it.

Chapter 4: How To Perform Astral Projection

Astral travel is not an experience limited to people who are suffering from serious illness as what the media portrays. In fact, it is possible for people to practice astral travel at will as long as they train themselves. This chapter will discuss the steps on how to perform astral projection.

How to Prepare Yourself for Astral Projection

Before you do astral travel, it is important that you prepare yourself so that you don't encounter problems during your projection. People who embark with astral projection without doing the necessary preparations often find it difficult to project themselves or they may encounter entities that might not be able to deal with. This section will discuss what you need to know about what you need to do to prepare for astral projection.

Choose the right time for astral travel: While some people choose to do astral projection at night, some people start it during early morning when they are still drowsy. Some experts claim that it is easier to achieve the necessary relaxation as well as heightened awareness during early morning. Thus, it is important to choose the time of the day wherein you can easily fall into a deep relaxation mode.

Create the right atmosphere: It is important that you are fully relaxed before you do astral travel. Thus, it is crucial to create the right atmosphere by choosing a part of your house where you are completely comfortable. You can lie in your bed or sofa to feel relaxed. When doing astral travel, it is crucial that you remove all the necessary obstructions in your room. You can also draw the curtains in your room to filter noises from the outside.

Lie down: Position yourself comfortably by lying on your back. Close your eyes and clear your mind from any thoughts. Concentrate on the sensations going through your body. To help you relax further, flex your muscles and slowly loosen them. Breathe deeply and focus your mind on the rise and fall of your chest. Let yourself sink into relaxation.

Use a quartz crystal: To help you attain good positive vibration for your astral travel, it will also do you good if you use a quartz crystal. While lying on your back, old a crystal on your third eye which is the area just slightly above the center of your eyebrows. Feel the vibrations that will clear your head and envision yourself wrapped in a golden or white color. Slowly place the crystal on your chest or abdomen to protect you on your astral journey.

How to Move Your Soul Out Of Your Body

Once you are able to make yourself calm and relaxed, the next thing that you need to do is to focus your soul from moving out of your body to begin your astral journey. However, it is very difficult to pull out your soul from your body if you are not doing it right. This section will discuss what it is that you need to know in order to move your soul out of your body.

Reach a hypnotic state: The hypnotic state is termed as hypnagogic state. This is the state wherein your body is approaching a sleep-like state without losing your mind's consciousness. To do this, start at the edge of your wakefulness and sleep by keeping your eyes closed but letting your mind wander to any part of your body. Use your mind to flex that particular body part and visualize it moving until you think that it is indeed physically moving. Move to the rest of your body and do the same thing until you are able to move all of your body in your mind. Focusing on a particular body part until you can visualize it in your mind (even with eyes closed) will help you cast away all unnecessary thoughts that you are thinking.

Enter a state of vibration: Once you are able to move your whole body in your mind, you will be able to feel waves of vibrations at different frequencies coursing throughout your body. This is an indication that your soul is ready to leave your body. Do not be taunted with these vibrations as your fear might cause you to abort your thoughts from its meditative state.

Use your mind to move your soul out of your body: In your meditative state, imagine your whole body inside the room where you are currently in. Picture your soul moving and standing up away from your body. Get up from the bed and walk across the room. Look back and take a look of your body lying peacefully on the bed.

Return to your body: Remember that your soul will always be connected to your body through an invisible cord. Let this force guide you back to our body. Re-enter your body by picturing your astral self, lying on top of your physical body. Now move your fingers and toes physically and regain your consciousness.

You will know that you have successfully had an out-of-body experience when you successfully gaze down on your body from across the room and that you are still aware of your conscious self. This process highly discourages you from leaving your room and traveling in an astral plane. The purpose of this exercise is to teach you how to control your meditative state. Until you have full control of your ability to move your soul of your body, you need to constantly practice and that may still take a lot of time and practice.

How to Explore the Astral Plane

Once you can start projecting your soul out of your body, it is time that you practice astral travel in an astral plane. Traveling in an astral plane for the first time can be a scary thing to do. Remember that you will be traveling by yourself on an astral plane. This section will discuss on how you can explore the astral plane and have a meaningful time with this experience.

Make sure that you are really projecting your soul away from your body: As soon as you have mastered projecting your soul away from the body within a room, it is important that you confirm that you are really located in two separate planes. So the next time that you practice astral projection, walk into another room in the house without looking back at your lying body. Once you are in another room in your house, examine a specific object in the room and take a metal note of its shape, color and size. Go back to your physical body and wake up. Once you are fully awakened, go to the room where your astral body went and confirm the details of the object that you examined.

Explore other places further: Once you have confirmed the object from another room, you can explore further that are less familiar to you. Every time you go to a new place, examine a new object that you have never noticed before. After each session and once you go conscious, physically verify the details of the object that you have examined by your astral self. Once you have travelled to different places, you will become more confident with astral traveling.

Ask for protection from a divine being: Some people believe that astral travel is a dangerous thing to do even if you have a lot of experience traveling to new places. If you plan to take your astral travel to more unfamiliar places, it is important that you ask protection from a divine being to protect you from the entities that you will meet along your journey. It will also help if you imagine yourself being wrapped in a glowing light all throughout your journey to protect you from any negative energies from affecting your travel.

Other Things You Need To Know About Astral Travel

There are many things that you need to know about astral travel. Below are the other things that you need to take note about your astral travel experiences. Below are the things that you need to understand when it comes to astral travel.

The silver cord or force does not weaken through time contrary to what most people believe in. It is a pure energy thus it cannot be removed or eliminated. It can only be moved from one place to the other. It is a natural and all-healing power.

Although it cannot be broken, there are times that you will find it difficult to re-enter your body. This is especially true if your astral self spends too much time traveling. Do not worry though since your body and soul are both intrinsically entwined with each other that it will naturally come back when the time is right.

Always ask protection if you plan on traveling to new places. Starting out with a prayer before you perform a projection or envisioning yourself being encapsulated by light is a good way to protect yourself. The thing is that you need to be able to protect yourself all the time.

The most interesting part of astral travel is that you can interact with other astral projections and meet new astral travelers along the way.

You can also heal other people during your astral travel. Remember that the astral self is a form of pure healing energy so you can envision a very sick person and ask protection as well as healing from the divine being.

Chapter 5: Preparing For Astral Projection

As we discussed in the previous chapter, preparation is essential to having a safe and successful astral projection experience. The most important preparation one can do is to prepare mentally and spiritually for the journey, but there are ways to prepare your physical body for the experience, as well. The best experience will come when you take care of your whole self, mind, body, and spirit.

Make Sure Your Body Is Nourished

Leaving your body will take a higher toll on it than you might expect. If flying on an airplane can leave your body with jet lag, what do you think leaving it energetically will do? As tempting as it is to turn one's thoughts towards the spiritual realm and leave behind the world of the physical, you will be returning to this world and must prepare your physical body for the unexpected change.

Any psychic activity can leave you feeling drained and exhausted because you are training yourself to interact with energies that vibrate at a higher frequency than what you are used to. We'll look at different ways to raise your vibration in an upcoming section of this chapter, but before you can start the psychic and energetic part of the process, you must take care of your physical body first.

Before you settle in to begin your meditation, you'll want to make sure that your body is properly nourished and hydrated. The amount of energy you will expend could cause your blood sugar to drop suddenly, and if you're running on empty, this could compromise your ability to maintain full control over the astral projection process. Expending so much energy without helping your body to get the nourishment it needs could lead to fatigue and even illness. It is far better to take the time to eat and hydrate before you begin than to spend several days recovering from your astral travel.

When preparing your pre-astral travel meal, take care to avoid foods that can cause upset stomach, indigestion, or gas. Anything that causes discomfort to your physical body will keep your attention focused on the physical world, making it difficult to depart into higher spiritual realms. A simple, digestion-friendly meal is best.

Many people choose to avoid eating meat before undertaking any psychic activity. Meat is believed to be of a denser vibration, and a meat-heavy diet can prevent one from fully raising their vibration to the appropriate level. Fruits, vegetables, nuts, grains, and any other food that comes from the Earth is said to be best for preparing the body for psychic activity.

You'll also want to make sure that your body is properly hydrated. Avoid caffeine, as that can prevent you from relaxing enough to slip into a trance state. Don't drink so much that your body will pull your astral self back to take a bathroom break. If you do feel your body pulling on you when you're out exploring the cosmos, whether for a bathroom break or because you're becoming excessively hungry or thirsty, remember that this is the body you'll have to live with for the rest of your life, so it's best to attend to its needs first.

Clearing Your Mind with Meditation

You'll get nowhere fast when attempting astral projection unless you know how to properly clear your mind with meditation. Any distractions can keep your energy tied to the physical world, with all its obligations and cares. Unless you can release these noisy thoughts, you'll have no choice but to remain with them.

The best way to clear your mind and to teach your body to relax enough that it can sleep while your mind stays awake is to focus on your breathing. To begin, inhale a deep breath to the count of seven. Feel your chest expand fully with your breath. Hold for four counts, then exhale to the count of eight. Push every ounce of air out of your lungs so that your next inhalation will bring in new, fresh energy to rejuvenate you. The deep breathing and counting will bring your attention to your physical body and help you center your awareness.

As your mind clears, release all tension from your body. Allow your muscles to relax as your body sinks into your chair or cushion. Beginning at your feet, relax every muscle, bone, and tendon. Move slowly up to your ankles, your shins and calves, your knees, your thighs, and so on all the way up to the crown of your head.

Once you are fully relaxed, practice staying in this clear state for as long as you can. Anytime your mind begins to pick up its usual mental chatter, take deep breaths again using the 7-4-8 count to clear again. This clear, relaxed state is where you'll need to be when it's time to begin your astral projection experience.

Raising Your Frequency

Everything in the universe is made of energy. Even the atoms that make up physical matter move around within themselves, vibrating at an imperceptible speed. Through their experiments, quantum physicists have found that some atoms vibrate at a faster rate, or a higher frequency, than others. The denser elements such as metals vibrate slower than gaseous elements like helium and hydrogen.

Modern spiritualists believe that the energetic realms of spirit vibrate at an even higher frequency than the highest of the physical realm because they are made of pure energy and have no dense physical vibrations to slow them down. Thus, in order to interact with these realms, we must raise our own vibrations.

Diet and meditation are two of the most straightforward techniques for raising your vibration. Practicing loving kindness towards yourself and others is another great way to raise the frequency of your vibrations. It is believed that the higher the frequency, the closer towards harmony the energy of a person or place. Denser vibrations are associated with chaos and negative emotions. The amazing ice crystal experiments of Masaru Emoto provide spectacular evidence to support this claim.

Energy healing, such as reiki, and sound healing, such as crystal bowls and gongs, can also raise your vibration. Listening to CDs with these beautiful sounds and receiving a reiki healing session or learning to do reiki yourself are excellent ways that you can raise your frequency with energy and sound.

Setting Your Intentions

Before you begin your astral projection ceremony, you'll want to set firm intentions about where you want to go, whom you want to meet, and what your goals are. The astral and etheric realms are vast beyond imagining, and it can be easy to get sidetracked. A playful but mischievous being who has no concept of your healing work could easily pull you off course, and while you may have tons of fun, you could also find yourself disappointed if you did not meet your goals in the way that you wish.

As we'll see in the chapter on protecting yourself in the astral realm, setting intentions also plays a huge role in establishing boundaries and staying safe. Before you begin your astral projection meditation, you'll want to state aloud and/or write your intentions down in your journal. Not only will this help keep you focused and on track, but you'll also be able to look back and see which of your goals you've accomplished, and which may need more attention.

Practicing with Guided Meditations

Before you begin the process of entering your first astral projection experience, it is highly recommended that you practice following simpler guided meditations first. Getting into the habit of working with guided meditations will prime your mind to slip into the focused meditative state necessary for successful astral projection.

You can find plenty of guided meditations available for free on YouTube, and there are countless books available on the topic. Find meditations that will help you work through the deeper issues of your unconscious mind. Being in touch with your unconscious self will greatly aid you on your journeys in the astral realm.

Taking the time to prepare yourself before you begin astral projecting by following all of these steps will equip you to handle whatever you may experience or encounter, and will ensure that your efforts will be successful.

Chapter 6: How To Experience Astral Projection And Never Be The Same Again

Astral Projection can be accomplished in several ways. Most people experience it when dreaming, meditation or being hypnotized. Some have even experienced astral projection during a relaxation time. Philosophers believe that while experiencing an astral projection, you will be tethered to the physical body by an invisible silver cord, such as an umbilical cord that tethers a mother to her child.

Method 1

With method 1 you will sit very still and go into a deep trance. You will know you are ready when you are so relaxed that you can no longer feel your physical body. Once you are in the trance, concentrate on your Chakras and imagine that you are being held there by those chakras, coming from the four corners of your body.

Imagine like a door knob you are turning your chakras in reverse which will release your chakras and help you to astral project. This is the basic concept of releasing your astral being in the astral plane by stretching each corner of your being out into the world, it is like your spirit or soul is slowly being released from your body.

Method 2

With this method you will lie down and relax, once relaxed and in a trance you will picture yourself floating away. As you lay perfectly still, imagine your left arm rising up above your physical body, then imagine every other limb rising until you are floating above your body. Continue to do this meditation exercise as often as possible and eventually you will astral project. Each time you let your limbs begin to float above, you helps you get closer and closer to an astral projected state of mind.

Hypnosis

Astral projection can also be accomplished by hypnosis. When you hypnotize someone you are using a mind trick to put them into a relaxed, sleep state, where you can travel back into time and examine your past lives. Many people swear that past lives are evident in your fears that you have today, such as, a child afraid of water may have drowned in a pool, lake, or river. Some people believe that they have watched themselves die, or have seen themselves as kings and queens, or aristocrats. Whoever you are in the past or the future, astral projection can help you make choices about your life that has been too difficult to make. Hypnosis will help you to understand your fears and explain things about yourself that you otherwise would be confused on. When you are hypnotized you go under a deep trance, which is similar to a meditative state. While under this deep trance you are subject to visiting a past life, or being programed to act in a certain way, such as barking when you hear a bell ring. Hypnosis is a long practiced medicine that has made headway in the science of helping people to stop smoking, over eating, or to understand and remember past experiences that have been blocked from their memories.

Relaxed state of mind

Many people say that when you are in a completely relaxed state of mind you can experience an astral projection best. They suggest trying first thing in the morning or right before you fall asleep. These are times when your body and mind are totally at rest and are more accepting of astral projecting. By relaxing your body and mind you can experience a different state of mind, and explore and learn about the astral planes.

Once you reach astral projection

Once you have reached an astral projection state you are actually floating in the fifth dimension which happens to be the astral plane between life and death.

The astral plane is a place where you go when you are completely relaxed, it is where people go when they pass away, and it is where angels and demons reside. When in an astral projected state of mind you learn many things about yourself, you learn what your dreams are, your hopes, and your purpose in life is revealed, this is why many people try astral project. They feel like they can learn private things about their being that they otherwise would not have known. They feel that they learn the purpose of life, the truth behind reality, and the faults that they do not truly know about themselves that are inside them.

Dreaming about Flying

Dreaming about flying or falling or anything of the like is not considered astral projection. When you wake up, then fall back to sleep, you will experience astral projection from the lucid dreaming state. When you trigger your lucid dreaming, you will also develop a form of paralysis that helps you to astral project. When your body is so relaxed that you feel paralyzed then your mind has the opportunity to release your astral being from your physical being so that you can float around in an astral plane.

Chapter 7: Preparing For Astral Projection And Travel

Have you clicked by now that there is a difference between the terms astral projection and astral travel or do they come across as synonymous? Of course, the two are closely related but we need to understand them well so that we can get the proper picture in our minds when we are discussing them. After all, they both have everything to do with visualization – mental images as opposed to the physical.

Astral projection precedes astral travel in occurrence. This you can understand when we describe astral projection as the skillful act of projecting your entire consciousness away from your physical body and getting it to enter and settle in your astral body. Astral travel, on the other hand, is the art of movement as an astral body. So for your astral body to make astral travels and interact with other astral bodies, you have first to be successful in your astral projection.

It is worth pointing out that though the two terms – astral projection and astral travel – may sound kind of mystical, they represent things that anyone is capable of doing. You just need to be sincere about wanting to have an astral experience. The key thing you need to master is concentration. Once you are able to concentrate on whatever step you are taking in the process of astral projection, you can focus on your intended shift from your physical being to astral existence. That is why you need to master the art of meditation.

Some Helpful Meditation Tips

Using the 4-Fold Breath

This is a breathing technique used in meditation, where you undergo four crucial steps. Although this is not the only meditation technique that there is, every other that you find is based on this one. That is why it is so important that you master it. It succeeds in getting you in a stable mood and in a position to concentrate fully on the mission before you.

Here is how you prepare for the meditation session:

Wear clothes that are loose fitting; clothes you feel comfortable in

Take a sitting position that you are comfortable in, and one that is unlikely to draw you to sleep. Often people opt to sit some place flat and with their back upright.

Sit within an area that is free from distraction – whether it is from noise or movements.

Here are the four steps to follow in your meditation:

Take four seconds to draw air in through your nose – inhalation

Take another good four seconds holding that air in – holding your breath

Take yet another four seconds breathing out the air, still through your nose – exhalation

Suppress further breathing for four seconds after that exhalation.

Your one session is up. Do not fret if you fail to get it right in your first attempt. It gets easier with practice. Remember that in astral projection, relaxation is important; and if you get upset with yourself for not doing your meditation right you will be sabotaging your own efforts. Just try and ignore everything else and focus strictly on your breathing. And if you get distracted, adopt the attitude of better luck next time – and you try again.

For how long should you practice this meditation?

Well, the period recommended is 5min – 10min long sessions of meditation. And you are advised to take such a session once every day. Then later, as you become comfortable and proficient in the meditation technique, you can prolong your sessions to something like 20min – 30min each. Since you want to succeed fast in mastering this meditation technique, register in your mind the basics – keeping your mind clear of distracting thoughts; ensuring your breathing pattern is regular; and that you are keeping to your set rhythm of breathing.

Keep a Record of What Works For You

It is important to keep a record of what transpired during each meditation session, especially when you are a beginner, because you want to establish the conditions and circumstances that are best suited for you. For example, you need to note in writing the time when you did your meditation; what the weather was like; the kind of clothes you had on; and even the kind of scents that were around you.

One thing you need to know is that there are people who are good at astral projection but they have realized they have trouble meditating in stormy weather. Others just cannot concentrate at certain times of the day. Still others meditate best in the evening and in full moon. You too need to identify what works for you so that you can time your meditation sessions accordingly.

Initial Steps of Astral Projection

First of all, you need to master a good breathing technique like the one explained above. Just before you begin your astral projection session, do this meditation for about 10 minutes.

Practice energizing your chakras or revitalizing your energy centers. You can consider this another form of meditation. Although there are things that you do without giving much thought to, when you are preparing for an experience in astral projection there are things you need to consciously do to ensure your chakras are well stimulated. Remember you need the energy through your chakras flowing well and in a balanced manner if you are to succeed in astral projection.

Ways to stimulate your chakras:

Regulate your thoughts

Thoughts, just in case you didn't know, come in form of energy. And it does not matter if the thoughts are emotional or just mental; they are connected to your chakras. So whatever thoughts you have do have influence over the way energy flows through your chakras. If you are churning negative thoughts from your mind, you end up being tense and either with energy levels being low or your energy flow being blocked in some areas. Yet you already know that you need to be relaxed when you are preparing for an astral projection. And you need your mind to be alert.

Seek some sunlight

Who doesn't know that the sun gives us energy? And not just us as human beings – every living thing benefits from the sun's natural energy. For you and me, the seven color spectrum from the sun is what penetrates our bodies to re-energize our different chakras with the respective auras. That is why there is emphasis on you getting some sunshine regularly. And supposing there is no sunshine where you live? That's no problem. Experts reckon a light bulb emitting the full spectrum of colors is good enough. So connect one to a light source and your chakras will be re-energized.

Eat different colored foods

The reason for this suggestion is that each color you find in vegetables, fruits or even flowers is representative of some form of natural energy matching some aura. And you, obviously, need the natural energy in its variety in order that your energies can be balanced. When you have all the necessary energies, there is good balance amongst the different chakras and you are in a good position to project in an astral way.

Do some visualization

This is not something really new but a form of yoga, where you breathe and meditate as you visualize specific colors. If, for instance, you think a certain chakra is weak or if you are feeling unwell in particular areas that are associated with a particular chakra, visualize the aura color that goes with that chakra and you will revitalize that chakra.

Use healing crystals

Healing crystals are great for boosting your energy. Different crystals emit different energies depending on their layers of crystallization which are responsible for their specific colors. Just to give you an idea of how helpful crystal are, wearing a moonstone or carrying one with you has been known to heighten your spiritual awareness. And this would be very helpful in a situation where you want to leave your physical existence and traverse the astral arena.

Do some color bathing

Here what is recommended is the use of color energy bath products. You essentially use these products to change the color of your bath water, and then you lie in the water and let your body sap up the energies from the water. Remember that water is good at conducting energy and so whatever energy the bath product introduces into the water ends up merging with your own energy, giving it a good boost and balance.

If you are looking forward to being passionate and enthusiastic about your astral experience, you may choose color red for your water. And if your heart is feeling somewhat faint, then what suits you is a green colored bath product to introduce the green color into your bath water. Then your 4th chakra, which is responsible for your heart's performance, will be opened better and vibrations enhanced.

Enjoy some aromatherapy

This simply means using some genuine essential oils. These are actually made of pure essence extracted from plants and sometimes flowers. You are supposed to mix a little of your chosen essential oil with some carrier oil before you use it. Often, however, people use essential oils in baths. And you are advised not to apply an essential oil directly onto your skin without first diluting it with a carrier oil otherwise you could suffer irritation. Carrier oils, just to refresh your memory in case you need it, are oils extracted from kernels; nuts; or even seeds. They themselves may be therapeutic too but our purpose here, we are more concerned with their role as carriers of the energy boosting essential oils.

You can use music and even dance

Yes, you can dance your way into relaxation and into enthusiasm and energy. One thing you need to know is that every music note is associated with a certain color, and as you know, different colors correspond to different chakras. There are some music notes you can play and find yourself emotionally stimulated. Other music notes stimulate you mentally; while others stimulate you physically.

For instance, just listening to primal music, or dancing to it – like music with drum beats – ends up energizing you physically. Such music is associated with your first chakra; the root chakra. And the root chakra, the one found at the base of your spine, is in charge of your physical energy and your stability. It is also the one that enhances your strong will. Of course you need to be strong willed to succeed in astral projection; otherwise you'll give up after a few attempts if you don't succeed right away.

Mastering the art of toning sounds

Here, think in terms of surrounding yourself with nice cool sounds. Whether these are musical sounds or others, the idea is to overwhelm any distracting sounds that may penetrate your area of meditation; or the place that you have chosen for your astral projection. You can even make vocal sounds of your own that vibrate at a common frequency with particular parts of your body. This is all in a bid to tone those organs so that they can work optimally.

And there is surely a lot more you could do to stimulate your chakras including using color filters to tone your body; energizing water with solar energy from direct rays of the sun; use of therapeutic eye glasses; selecting colored décor for use in your room; choosing clothing that improves your mood and makes you feel energized; and surrounding yourself with colorful art.

Get your astral energy flowing

At this juncture, you have done your basic meditation and your body is ready to move to the next level; that one of letting go of your astral body. It is now time to go to the next level in meditation, where your consciousness is now on your astral energies; trying to help your astral body take off and venture into the astral realm of existence.

Embark on astral projecting

This is the stage that marks your ultimate success at astral projection. Here, you let your astral body loose and you move to wherever it takes you. You are now at the point where you can see yourself as a separate being, either laying the way you are on the bed or wherever you may be, or even doing different things as your astral body observes.

Chapter 8: Different Ways To Astral Travel

People can achieve an astral projection through many ways. There is no single method that can work for everyone. These techniques are aimed to separate the astral self from the body and induce an astral experience.

The Rope technique

This astral projection technique is pioneered by Robert Bruce. This is particularly helpful to beginners in astral projection. The rope technique is prescribed to be one of the easiest ways to astral project.

The first step is to calm the mind and body. Mediate and create a series of deep breaths. One way to relax the body is by tensing muscles and releasing them one by one. After being fully relaxed, the person has to enter a hypnotic state that places the mind at the edge of sleep. Focus on an object until it is memorized. Look around with eyes closed and gaze into the darkness. A light pattern may appear but this should be ignored. Once these light patterns disappear, the mind has already entered a deeper state of consciousness.

The most vital step in this technique is when the person starts to feel vibrations. This means that the astral self is beginning to separate from the physical body. An individual has to let go and acknowledge these vibrations. Focus on the vibrations and use willpower to control them.

When the vibrations started to be more controllable, imagine a long rope hanging above. Without moving and keeping eyes closed, feel the body reaching toward the rope. Once the rope is reached, bring the hand back down to the physical body. Practice several times before attempting to raise the whole body into the rope. Concentrate in using the rope to climb out from the physical body and do not stop until the astral self is separated from the physical body.

This method does not require visualization. The person do not actually visualize the rope, they just have to know where it is. An important thing in the rope technique is to not break concentration while climbing up the rope. It is important to ignore all sensations that might cause distraction.

The lift and roll technique

The lift and roll technique will create an etheric projection. A deep relaxation must be achieved first; the person must imagine himself floating upwards away from the body. It would be helpful to think of happy thoughts while doing this technique. It can also help if an imaginary help is visualized. For example, one may imagine a flock of birds trying to lift the body up. When vibrations started to happen, they should be ignored completely. Just focus on visualizing the separation of the astral body to the physical body. Once the separation is complete, an overwhelming sense of freedom closes in on the spirit.

One variation of the floating technique is the roll out technique. This works similarly except instead of floating, the astral body is separated by rolling sideways. Start by gently rocking from side to side then increase momentum until the astral body is rolled out of the physical self.

The Anchor technique

The idea of the anchor technique is to imagine an anchor point outside of the physical body and use it as leverage to separate from the physical body.

The Fixed Anchor technique

Once the person has reached a state of trance, focus on a point outside the body. The individual can focus on space or an object and imagine this anchor to be as solid as possible. The focus point should be immovable and fixed where it is. No amount of mental concentration should be able to make it move. When the mind is ready, reach out to grab the focus point and pull. Since the focus point is fixed, the person will now start to separate from the physical body.

The Moving Anchor

Imagine a familiar object floating 6" in front. Imagine the object pulling the body in a magnet-like manner. Move the object closer and feel the pull getting stronger. Move the object back and feel the magnet-like pull weaken. Repeat the process until the whole body is comfortable to separate. The object should be able to pull the astral self away from the body.

The Mirror technique

The mirror technique is an effective way to prepare an individual for an out of the body experience. Begin by placing a mirror in a location which can be easily viewed without any physical movement. Look in the mirror and memorize the image. Pay attention even to small details. Once the entire self is memorized, the person must close his eyes and imagine himself at the opposite side of the room. Try to move arms and leg, walk around the room and feel the sensation of movement without a physical body. Practice the technique until it gets familiar. Slowly begin to open the imaginary eyes. Look around the room, this might feel like pretence at first but after some time the ability to see beyond the restrictions of the body will sharpen. The key to this method is practice. If opening imaginary eyes is too difficult, focus on other senses like touch. Try to forget the physical body and focus attention into the astral self. Slowly, as the body goes to sleep, all the awareness will now transfer to the astral body.

Partner Technique

The Partner technique is a variation of Christos technique that was originally developed by G.M. Glaskin. This method is ideal for partners, couples and groups. Silence is an important element to this technique. The partner lies on his back with eyes closed and the head should be placed to the north. Make him relaxed as possible. Begin massaging his ankle bones in a circular motion, after two minutes, quietly place four fingers on the forehead and rub in a circular pattern. Slowly increase the pressure and speed until the partner reports a loud buzzing sound then stop.

The verbal guided meditation should be next. Speak in a slow relaxing voice and guide the partner into taking deep breaths and feeling the energy transfer from the top of his head to his feet. As the partner feel the energy at the bottom of his feet, coach him to imagine the energy extending for four inches. Repeat this method until he is comfortable with the sensation. Duplicate the process by transferring the energy on top of the head and visualizing it extend for four inches. Once comfortable, coach the partner by telling him to feel the weightlessness of his body. Take time and enjoy each sensation and feel free to enhance visualization and meditation.

The Yo-yo

Before going to sleep choose a familiar spot in the bedroom and memorize every detail of it. Stand on this spot and memorize the sensation of being there. Go to bed and lie down then shift awareness into the target. Imagine being right at the spot for just a second then bring back awareness to the body. Bounce awareness back and forth between the body and the target at one second interval. The person should start feeling vibrations just like in those felt in using the rope technique.

Free Fall

The free fall technique starts just like any astral method. A person should be completely relaxed and enter a state of trance and imagine falling down with incredible speed. Associate all the feeling related to falling. If it is done right vibrations can be felt along with the sensation of being lost in space. Continue visualizing and when the astral self is close to separating with the body, imagine a sudden collision to the ground, this can cause the astral self to completely separate from the body.

Exhaustion

This astral technique is done by letting the body fall into deep sleep because of exhaustion. A person should resist sleeping until he can no longer keep the eyes open then lie down in an uncomfortable position. Try to retain consciousness while the body falls asleep. Once the vibrations start, imagine getting up without using any muscle. The astral body should be able to separate easily this way.

Forced sleeping

This method is best performed in the morning after waking up. Eyes should be kept closed and the body should stay motionless at all times. Allow the body to fall asleep for at least 10 seconds. This will trick the brain into thinking that the body is going back to sleep. This will put the person at a state of sleep paralysis, after 10 seconds of sleep, aggressively attempt to separate from the physical body.

Straining the brain

This is one unusual method to achieve an out of the body experience. Imagine squeezing the brain inside the head and feel the tension in brings. This will cause vibrations coupled with the sensation of falling down. Keep straining the brain until the astral self completely separates from the body.

Tunnel

During a trance, try imagining a long dark tunnel. At the end of the tunnel is a light. A person must imagine himself flying through the tunnel like an airplane ready to take off. When vibrations starts to happen, ignore them and concentrate on the white light at the end of the tunnel. As the consciousness reaches the white light projection will start.

Running

Imagine yourself running as fast as possible. Good visualization is not necessary; just concentrate on the sensation of running. Imagine a tension in the muscles as running starts to speed up but keep the real muscles relaxed. When vibrations occur wait until it has become intense then imagine hitting a wall in front. The collision will cause an out of the body experience.

Eye movement

Perform a quick left to right eye movement. This would cause the focal point to be off balance and will cause astral projection.

Dot on the forehead

The focal point of humans is usually located in between the eyes. That is where consciousness resides. A person must concentrate on this spot and fully transfer all awareness there. This might cause vibrations and a sensation of floating. Keep concentration on the focal point until the astral body separates.

Phantom wiggling

Wiggle hand or foot and feel the movement without actually performing it physically. Continue to do this until vibration occurs then intensify the wiggling motion until projection is achieved.

Recall

The recall method can only be done by a person who has already successfully attempted astral projection. When sleep paralysis is achieved, begin imagining the last astral projection and visualize it as vivid as possible. Remember what vibrations feel like and recall all sensations associated with it. This method might lead to another astral projection.

Vibration Field

Lie in bed with eyes closed and visualize a field of energy vibrating. Slowly imagine moving the energy towards the body. This white pulsating ball of energy should touch the body and absorb the vibration. The vibration will transfer into the body and this can trigger an out of the body experience. Try to intensify the vibrations and simply roll out of the physical body.

Progressive separation

This is a French method that is best used when the body is in vibration state already. Concentrate all effort on one foot and try to wiggle it. Do the same thing with the other foot and repeat the process for the entire body. If the method is done right, the person will completely separate from the body.

Tornado

This method is done when the body is in a deep state of relaxation try imagining being in the eye of a storm which is spinning incredibly fast. Feel all the sensations associated with it. This might cause hallucinations and vibration which will lead to astral projection. When this happens allow the tornado to release the body.

Astral Arms

This method is done by visualizing the arms slowly moving out of the body. Push the arms out of the body as hard as possible and drag the whole body with it. Concentrate on the visualization and not the physical movement. The body might sway a little but do not be distracted and concentrate on separating the astral self.

Chapter 9: Your First Astral Projection

Starting out with astral projection can be easy for some people and for others it can be harder. One of the main things that you need to overcome is your fear of astral projection, which is quite natural as it is unknown to you at the present time. Most people have a degree of fear of the unknown and this book plus some practise will help you overcome it.

A study was done by The Canterbury Institute with over 2,000 people practising astral projection and none of them reported any negative effects even when they were interviewed again three years later on.

To perform this technique you are going to need a room that is quiet where you won't be disturbed for the duration of your practise. Switch off your cell phone, unplug your landline and turn the lights down – you want the room to be dim but not black. Make sure your bladder is empty and that your clothing isn't tight.

Lie down comfortably and relax your body. This is an important first step as you need to be both physically and mentally relaxed. The easiest way to do this is to do a progressive muscle relaxation and some deep breathing. Start relaxing your body at your head and work down your body a bit at a time, relaxing everything as you go. Breathe deeply and evenly as you relax your body and you will soon be ready for astral projection.

Let yourself relax until you enter a stage close to sleep known as the hypnagogic state. One way to do this is to keep your upper arm on the bed and lift your forearm off the bed. As you fall asleep your arm will fall which will disturb you and wake you. With practise you will not need to use your arm to enter the hypnagogic state.

Another method of doing this is to concentrate your attention on a single object and then when other images start to come in to your thoughts you have entered the hypnagogic state. Do not interact with these images, but just passively watch them.

After you have entered the hypnagogic state you need to deepen the state some more. Just keep yourself relaxed and with your eyes closed look at the blackness that is in front of you. You may notice some light patterns as you do so. These are just neural discharges and can be ignored and will, after a while, stop.

Now you need to relax even further to such a state where you lose the awareness that you have a body. It's a state where you are in a void and the only stimulation you are aware of is your own thoughts.

This next step is the most important and the part that a lot of people struggle with. You need to enter a state of vibration which is typically when projection starts. You could feel this either as a mild tingling or as if electricity is flowing through your body. What causes these is a bit of a mystery but it is suspected to be the astral body attempting to leave your physical form.

You can help this to happen by laying down with your head in the north and your feet in the south – this seems to help kick this state off. Repeat to yourself that you are going to remember everything that happens and it will be for your higher good.

Concentrate on the void that you are in whilst deeply relaxed and focus your attention on a point around twelve inches in front of your forehead. Then next change your point of reference to a position about six feet away from your forehead.

Turn your point of reference through ninety degrees upwards, which can be done by visualizing a line parallel to the axis of your body. Focus your attention here and reach out mentally for the vibrations mentioned earlier. You may not have a full understanding of them but you will know exactly when you have touched them.

Practice controlling these vibrations by mentally pushing them from your head through your body to your toes so they produce vibrational waves that go from your head to your feet. Concentrate on pushing these vibrations down your body to create a wave effect. Practice this until you care able to make these waves happen on demand. Having control of this state is vital if you are planning on leaving your body.

Now it is time to partially separate from your body and you need to keep your thoughts firmly focused on leaving your body. Do not let your mind wander as stray thoughts could cause you to lose control.

Extend a limb of your astral body until it comes in contact with the wall nearest to your bed where you are lying. Feel it rest against the wall and then push it through the wall. Return it back so it is back with the physical limb. Take a break and then repeat it again.

Now you need to dissociate from your body and separate the astral and the physical bodies. One way to do this is to think about getting lighter and lighter and how nice it is to float upwards and out of your physical body. Keep this in your mind and do not let any stray thoughts distract you. As you keep focusing on the feeling of floating you will leave your body.

An alternative way to do this is either the roll-out or rotation method which you do when you have achieved the vibrational state. Try to roll over, just as if you were rolling over in bed, but do not try to do it physically. Twist your body from your head and you will typically roll your astral body out of your physical body. Then you can think of floating upwards and you will float up and away from your body.

This is one of the best methods for leaving your body, though in the next chapter you will learn some additional methods that you can use.

Chapter 10: Meditation And Hypnosis

Meditation has a plethora of benefits that can help you with your most complex issues. One that you might be struggling with at the moment is the ability to fall asleep and stay asleep.

Benefits of Meditation in Your Daily Life

As individuals, the first thing that we all crave in life is – peace.

But, peace is a broad term, and one that leads to an endless list of questions.

How do we define peace?

What gives us peace?

And most importantly why do we crave it?

All of these questions are pertinent, and all of them have weight. You will begin to realize it is even more as you embark on your personal journey into the human mind, in search of it. As you seek peace however, it is important that you first try to understand how the human mind works and more importantly how meditation has multiple positive effects on the human mind, body and soul.

Meditation: A Brief History

While we think of mental health and mental development and automatically look to meditation as the perfect solution, it does beg the question - where did meditation come from? How long has it been around? Where did it originate? Interestingly, most of these questions lack a clear definitive answer even today, thousands of years since the practice was first adopted.

Some scholars have claimed that meditation, in some form or another, has existed from the beginning of humanity. However, if you are looking for a more definitive answer, India is a good place to start. In this country, most commonly associated with meditation, Vendatism has been around since 1500 BC. In China, Taoist meditation also dates back to the 5th and 6th centuries. Some scholars have dated meditation practices in the region as far back as 5,000 - 6,000 BC.

In the west, meditation didn't quite come about until the 1700s, by way of a multitude of texts on Eastern Philosophy. It wasn't until Swami Vivekananda, a Hindu monk, presented a speech at the Parliament of Religions in 1893 that this massive wave of interest in meditation brought us to where we are today.

Building Self-Awareness

For starters let's focus on self-awareness.

Take a minute and honestly ask yourself how aware you are of how your body reacts to specific situations. How do you react to light? How do you react to fear? How do you react to happy events? Take a minute and identify each of these physical manifestations of your mind and evaluate them – why do you react in this way? Have you always acted in the specific manner? What has changed, if anything?

You may notice that as you go through these questions in your mind, other questions and thoughts will enter your mind that you didn't anticipate. This is actually very typical and natural. Often times even if you think that a specific thought or specific trigger will cause your mind to think or work in a specific manner in reality it doesn't necessarily process the information in any specific way. This is why reverse psychology works on certain individuals and backfires on others – not all people react to the same form of stimulus in the exact same manner. Meditation allows you to practice introspection and truly identify how your mind reacts to specific triggers. It's almost as if your mind is doing a mental inventory of how you think, how you process, and most importantly how you react.

Try to think of meditation as a form of mental yoga – here the objective is to forge a stronger link between the mind and body. This is to ensure that your mind is more aware of how your body is responding specifically to cues. Meditation helps us understand our own individual sense of awareness. Helping ground us in the present moment allows us to act and think in a way that keeps us in the present.

Reducing Stress and Anxiety

This is just one benefit —meditation is not intended to simply enhance one's sense of self. In fact a major reason why so many people get involved in meditation, is because they wish to use the practice to cure themselves of unwanted stress and anxiety that they might be dealing with.

Let's simplify this, shall we?

Why do you think you are invested in meditation?

What do you feel unsure or nervous about starting your meditation program?

Try answering this instead – in the past week what are five negative things that have impacted the way you act, think and react? Make a short list in a separate journal. Have you listed them for yourself? Good! Now ask yourself how often one of these thoughts has controlled your mind. Let's say you feel unhappy at work – how often have you thought of quitting? A lot? How often do you think about how badly you want to change jobs? Almost always?

Most importantly how often have you done something that would help you change your job, or extract yourself from that toxic work environment? Odds are you just said never very quietly under your breath. Whether or not you feel like you are ready to admit your thoughts to other people, you yourself know exactly how often you are sometimes even obsessing over the negatives in your life. Do you ever wonder why you don't feel comfortable telling other people how often these negative thoughts come to your mind?

Think about it - if you don't like admitting how you are thinking, odds are that you already know, subconsciously or at some level, that what you are doing isn't good for you. Always keep in mind that while negative things will continue to happen in your life, how far you allow that negativity to spread into your personal space is a decision that you are making constantly. There is always a more productive way to deal with negative thoughts – if you feel you are stuck in a bad job, instead of obsessing over the negative features of the job entails, train your mind to focus on the way out. Line up new job interviews, consider talking to the human resources department or a supervisor; the point here is to actually actively do something instead of just letting things happen to you.

Taking control of the negativity that surrounds you is a key part of ensuring that you lead a healthier and happier life, because this negativity is what breeds stress and causes anxiety to build in your mind. So, if you really want to live a stress free, healthier and most importantly, happier life you are going to want to start by finding a way to reduce your stress levels, and train your mind to focus on productive activities, instead of the anxiety triggers that you have built for yourself.

Honing Mental Clarity

Another common issue many individuals tend to have to deal with is – the lack of clarity that is predominant in today's world. For the most part, research has shown that multiple mental disciplines, such as yoga and meditation, can help control the mind and even improve it. Conditions such as ADHD, which is a form of attention deficiency, have been known to show significant improvement with meditation and meditation based activities.

While it is common knowledge that physical exercise can help keep the body in shape, what people tend to forget is that the brain needs the exact same thing. Neuro exercises, or mental training activities can potentially keep our brain in shape, and can also weed out certain undesirable mental characteristics, such as depressive thoughts, or anxiety.

One of the fundamental issues currently being studied by scientists is the subject of neuroplasticity. What is neuroplasticity, you may ask? Well, simply put, scientists have begun to discover that, contrary to popular opinion, an individual's brain is not shaped at the time of their birth – in contrast the brain is actually constantly growing and learning, which is why it is possible to actually change our brains to specific forms of mental training. For example, one can retrain the brain to alter or improve multiple personality quirks, such as how attentive you are, how happy you are, how angry you are etc.

Instead of considering emotions such as happiness, or anger, or disappointment individual reactions, think of them as skills. You can train your mind so that you are more skilled at being happy or positive, although odds are you have subconsciously been training your mind to be the exact opposite. Neuroscientist Richard Davison, of the University of

Wisconsin, conducted a three-month research program on the impacts of the Vipassana form of Buddhist meditation that deals with increasing mental clarity, and improving sensory awareness. On completion, he found that volunteers who had received Vipassana meditation as a form of mental training, were much faster in their ability to identify and focus on detailed information. In contrast, individuals who had not participated in the training seemed less clear and less stable in their ability to retain information. Because of this, meditation is now being seen as a form of mental exercise that helps individuals take advantage of the plasticity of the human brain, in a quantifiable and scientific manner.

Building Focus and Fortitude

However, it is not just mental clarity that is affected by meditation. In fact, a large part of meditation deals with building focus. While the science of the issue has clearly established that meditation can help enhance mental clarity by playing with the neural plasticity of the mind, it also does so on a more chemical level by releasing specific hormones to help counter your stress levels.

When you are stressed out, your body releases certain hormones to let your mind know that it is overloaded. Once your mind starts to register that you are stressed out, the body then starts to release adrenaline because it thinks that your body now needs more energy to help get you through these backlogged tasks. The only problem here is that adrenaline can work against you. While theoretically adrenaline should be helping you to get better and to do your tasks quicker and better. Adrenaline serves an important function in our bodies, but unless we learn to control stress, adrenaline works against us. Instead of helping us get through stressful moments, excessive adrenaline instead increases anxiety, and multiplies our stress reaction.

Keep in mind the release of adrenaline in your body is a physical reaction to fear or danger, or some sort of immediate desperate need – this is a physical reaction, that has been passed on to us from our ancestors, who at the time needed that extra bit of energy to fend off predators or to stay alive. Now imagine having that level of pressure put on you every single day, because you are unable to distinguish between a life-and-death situation, and a workplace crisis. Your body simply doesn't know the difference.

This of course is where meditation steps in. Meditation gives us a sense of self worth and power, so that when we are faced with a challenge, we are not immediately dropping the ball and going into "danger" mode – instead we are calmly teaching ourselves to cope, which in turn allows our brain to focus and develop better coping strategies.

Have you ever given yourself a social media detox? Is your immediate reaction after you wake up to check Facebook? One of the first things you might want to do is slowly detach from your phone or the distractions of social media over the next seven days.

Meditation teaches your brain to do the exact same thing in terms of the topics on which you are focusing. By slowly teaching yourself to focus on the factors which you would like, such as positive outcomes, you simultaneously build your mental fortitude. You're training your brain to not go into panic mode at the slightest thing. At the same time, you are also teaching yourself how to react to those smaller, yet persistent mental problems that you find yourself facing on a daily basis. Win-win!

Emotional Intelligence

So, what else does meditation help with? Well, for starters, it is also an extremely important tool in the development of emotional intelligence. As you begin to become more aware of your own self and how you react to specific situations, you will also realize that you are attuned to how people around you react to those same situations. This form of awareness is also commonly known as emotional intelligence, and is currently considered to be of extremely high value. Indeed, some scientists have begun to prefer the evaluation of emotional intelligence over the evaluation of one intelligence quotient to determine a person's potential.

While you probably ask yourselves multiple times whether or not you are good enough or smart enough, odds are you probably don't ask yourself if you are compassionate enough or if you are a good listener. If you are familiar with the television program, The Big Bang Theory, you've probably seen that the protagonist Sheldon Cooper has been portrayed to be an individual with extremely high IQ, but extraordinarily low EQ factor. In later seasons, this impacts his career growth, as well as his personal life. This is actually extremely common - no matter how smart you are, in order to truly succeed in life, you will find that you will require a certain amount of emotional intelligence.

Start asking yourself the following questions to gauge what your emotional intelligence levels are:

1. Are you generally a calm person? Are you capable of maintaining this calm in stressful situations?

2. Would you consider yourself to be compassionate? Are you well attuned to the needs of others?

3. In your opinion, do you have a tendency to make good decisions?

4. Are you capable of listening to what other people have to say? Do you take people's opinion into consideration?

5. Do you believe that you have a positive influence on the people around you?

6. Are you an impulsive person? How impulsive do you consider yourself to be, on a scale of 1 to 10?

7. What is your standard mind-set – happy or sad?

Were the answers that you just provided generally negative in nature? If so odds are you have a low EQ, the good news is it doesn't really matter how low your EQ is, because you can actually build on your EQ levels through meditation. The act of meditation not only helps you detach from negative thoughts, it is also known to help you assess and attune yourself to the emotions of other people. Poker players for instance are known to have extremely high emotional intelligence levels; their advanced emotional intelligence is what allows them to 'read' emotions such as fear or hesitation in their opponents, which in turn enables them to make better plays.

But, most importantly, your emotional intelligence levels will help you deal with years of emotional baggage that have burdened your inner mind control. Gone are the days that you couldn't control your temper. With the help of meditation, you can now actively deal with your anxiety, your depression, and your negative thought patterns, replacing them with solid reasoning skills and problem-solving capabilities.

Relaxing the Mind

And finally, one of the least appreciated and yet possibly one of the most beneficial attributes of meditation – mental relaxation. Think about it...when was the last time you gave your brain a break. Keep in mind that going away on holiday does not count. When was the last time that you sat still for 15 minutes and did absolutely nothing? You didn't mentally list the tasks that you have to do, you didn't make decisions about what you're going to need for dinner. You didn't worry about ten different things that happened today – you literally did nothing.

Let's be honest, odds are it's been a while. Lucky for you, meditation is actually known to trigger the relaxation response in the mind, which means that any time you spend meditating is time you are spending allowing your brain to go into a state of absolute relaxation.

Why is this important? The more relaxed your brain is the easier it is for you to fall asleep, to manage your stress levels, and to reduce your anxiety. Think of it as your emotional balance, by relaxing your brain you are training it to maintain better emotional equilibrium, which in turn allows you to become a more balanced individual.

These are just some of the numerous benefits that are attached to meditation. Meditation is also known to enhance kindness in societies, and help individuals become more community minded. It also plays a strong role in fighting addictions; studies have shown that recovering alcoholics generally do much better when they receive meditative training. So, with all our doubts put to rest, the only question now is how do we do it, or more accurately how do we prepare for it?

Chapter 11: Techniques

As stated earlier, in order to achieve your out of body experience, you're going to have to completely relax your body and allow yourself to slip to that space that is between being awake and sleeping.

But, there are techniques that you can use in order to help you achieve that hypnotic like state and be able to experience astral projection. Not every technique will work for every person, but you can still try one or two to see if you can find one that works for you.

The Rope Technique:

Developed by Robert Bruce, this technique has been said to be one of the most effective techniques when it comes to astral projection. The key component of this technique is an invisible rope that is hanging from your ceiling.

The rope is going to exert pressure to a single point on your astral body in order to help force your soul and body apart. Using your imaginary hands (in your mind), you're going to grab the rope above you and pull yourself up. You're going to mimic the actions as if you are trying to climb that rope with your astral body.

There is a feeling of dizziness that you may feel and the more that you pull on the rope; the feeling of vertigo may become stronger.

However, you're going to need to keep climbing up until you begin to feel the vibrations. Every part of your body will seem as if it is vibrating and yet paralyzed at the same time. It is important that you concentrate on climbing the rope.

Do not stop!

At some point you will feel as though you have come free from your body and moved towards where the rope is hanging above your body. This is where your astral travel will begin.

Watch yourself go to sleep:

Just as I have stated before, lie on your back and relax your mind from any unwanted thoughts. Ultimately you're going to want your mind completely void of any thought so that you are able to achieve a state of total relaxation.

Convince yourself that you're going to watch yourself go to sleep. You need to keep the intent of what you're doing extremely clear and allow your body to sleep while you keep your mind alert. This is just like the hypnotic state that I have told you that you're going to have to enter in order to achieve astral projection.

While you do this, you're going to need to learn to recognize the strange but distinctive sensations that you're going to feel as you fall into that sleep state. It is important that you stay aware of everything as it unfolds. Your body is eventually going to begin to feel numb as well as your limbs feeling heavy.

As you pay attention to the different sensations that you are feeling as well as the vibrations that you're going to feel, you are going to visualize that you are getting up out of the bed in which you are laying. Try and visualize how it would actually feel to be able to float as you begin to find yourself outside of your body.

Out of body experience from lucid dreams: A lucid dream is a dream in which the dreamer is actually aware of what he or she is dreaming. If you're experiencing lucid dreams, then you have already achieved an out of body experience of some sort.

In order to achieve an out of body experience or a lucid dream, it is important that you truly desire to have it. Make sure that you do all the research possible to be able to achieve a lucid dream.

As you go through your day, keep telling yourself that you're going to have a lucid dream later that night and then you need to ask yourself if you are actually dreaming at that point in time.

Displaced-awareness:

This technique happens when you close your eyes and fall into the usual trance that you need to be in in order to achieve astral projection. While you do this, try and sense the entire room all at once. Feel everything about yourself from the shoulders up, as you are passive to what is going on.

Imagine that your soul is actually rotating by 180 degrees. At the time that you finish the mental rotation, your soul's head should then be where your feet are as well as your astral feet where your head is.

Holding onto this image and now visualize what the room looks like from this point of view.

Once you have grown comfortable with this, imagine that you are floating and chances are you are going to feel as though you have popped from your physical body.

The Jump Technique

Should you try this technique, you should remember that you could actually end up waking yourself from your dream and turn it into a lucid dream. But, in order for this to be done, you have to do this technique properly and well.

Just like the lucid dream technique, you need to constantly ask yourself if you are dreaming or not. Do not do this just to ask yourself the question, but ask because you truly want to know if what you're thinking or doing is a dream. It is imperative that you doubt that you are part of the reality that your body is part of.

So, in order to prove to yourself that you are not part of the physical world, you're going to "jump" and try and fly. If you're still stuck in the physical world than you will end up landing back on the ground as if you had physically jumped. However, if you have done this technique properly, you will find yourself defying gravity.

Chapter 12: Separating The Astral Self From The Physical Body

Once the individual has gotten the hang of moving his various body parts with the use of his mind, he can now start the process of separating the astral self from the physical body. This can be done in stages starting with focusing on the entire room. Though it would take time for the individual to be able to visualize the entire room where the astral projection is being conducted, he should eventually be able to see it in his mind's eye. The next step is to focus on moving his body up from the bed or the mat that he is lying in. The goal on this step is for the person to be able to stand up without the aid of any physical force, simply by using the boundless power of his mind.

Once he succeeds in getting his body to stand up, the next thing to do is for the person to try looking at his own physical body that is lying on the bed. To be able to do this, he must first try to move his body and walk from the spot where he is standing up. Once movement is achieved, he could then try to walk to the other end of the room and then turn back to look at the spot where his physical body is located. The success of this step can be gauged when the person starts to get the feeling that he is looking at his own body lying on the bed from the spot across the room where he was able to mentally move to. Once the individual has felt this, and experts guarantee that this would definitely be felt during the initial process of astral projection, then he can be sure that he has already reached the final stage of separating his astral self and can now move on towards trying to reach other aspects of the astral plane.

Though the steps discussed above seem simple enough, many astral projectors have reported that it can be quite difficult to reach the final stage of separating the astral body from the physical body. This is the main reason why the hypnotic state has to be undertaken in small stages and why the individual has to try to move his body starting with one small part at a time. It might actually take days to practice the mere act of mentally lifting the pinkie finger of one hand. But as soon as this smaller act of mental control is achieved, the individual might be able to flex or lift other body parts with more ease as he progresses in his journey towards the astral plane.

Experts in astral projection have identified the following as possible barriers for the achievement of a successful out-of-body experience or astral projection:

Disbelief. This is characterized by a person's thoughts that question his ability on actually being able to do it. The person himself could be the barrier to his own success when he possesses a subconscious disbelief that astral projection is at all possible.

Misconceptions. One of the most common myths about astral projection that has keep many people from trying to do it is the idea that the astral self can get lost in a dark maze inside the astral world that would keep him from getting back to the physical world. Popular entertainment hasn't helped much in dissolving this misconception due to movies that feature false ideas about astral projection. Experts in astral projection have stated that the astral self is connected by an invisible thread, the silver cord, to the physical body. There is nothing in any dimension on the astral plane that can dissolve or disconnect this cord, not even demons or malicious beings.

Reflex Problem. This often stems from the person's fear and would compel him to constantly check on his physical body while his astral body is in the astral plane. This would gradually induce him to lose his focus on the astral projection and cut the experience short for him. This reflex problem is more common among people who suffer from obsessive-compulsive behavior. They have the compulsion that everything has its own place and each part has its own function, and this makes it difficult for them to release their hard-earned self-control in order to unleash the freedom of their astral selves within their own minds.

These barriers can be successfully overcome by simply doing enough research on the topic of astral projection. Individuals who wish to be able to successfully reach the astral plane are also advised to speak with people who have already done it so that their questions can be personally answered by someone who knows exactly what he is talking about. On the other hand, the fear of getting completely disconnected from the physical body and getting trapped in the astral self can be eased by the certainty that the human soul or astral self is always connected to the physical body regardless of how far along in the astral plane he is at and how long he has been there. This connections is often called the 'silver cord' and experts believe that it is the force that guides the astral self-back to the physical body.

Once the silver cord has successfully initiated the astral self's reentry into the physical body, the individual is advised to test out his balance by wriggling his toes and flexing his fingers. This time, the movement has to be done physically instead of just mentally. People who have just come back from the astral plane are also advised to give themselves enough time to regain their full level of consciousness by not standing up too abruptly. They have to re-adjust their physical bodies to their surroundings so as to avoid getting disoriented.

Chapter 13: Remote Viewing

One of the most interesting applications of astral travel is remote viewing. This is something that takes training, time and practice, but it is something you can get started on fairly easily.

Remote viewing is something that is so interesting and has so much potential that during the Cold War, both the US and Russian governments conducted experiments in remote viewing in an attempt to spy on each other. The details of these experiments are closely guarded secrets, but both countries experimented heavily with this technique, which gives you an idea of the importance and power of this.

Once you have mastered astral projection and can leave your body whenever you want then you can start experimenting and learning remote viewing. Have a friend select some pictures that have clear lines, shapes or colors, e.g. shapes, animals and so on. Get them to paste these on to a piece of plain white paper and then seal each one individually in to a separate envelope that you can't physically see through. Each envelope should also be numbered on the outside in large, bold writing from one to the total number of envelopes.

Make sure the pictures aren't too complex but they are interesting enough to stick in someone's sub-conscious mind. Try to make sure that each picture is as different as possible from each other to help with this process. Initially you may only partly recall the details from the envelope, so clearly, different pictures will help you whilst you are learning to remote view.

When you are ready, pick an envelope and place it somewhere that you can astral travel to. Enter the astral plane and go to the location of the envelope and attempt to see what is inside. Once you have done this, return to your body and write down what you saw in the envelope and then either yourself or your friend can check it.

An alternative method for this is to pick an envelope and sit down somewhere quiet with a few pieces of paper. Write Target 1 at the top of a piece of paper, put the first envelope in front of you and start to relax deeply. Try to focus on the envelope and perceive what is inside it. Record any impressions you get from the envelope.

Remember that you have a lot of mental noise anyway in your mind which is why it is important you learn to quieten your mind. It can be difficult, at least until you get used to it, to separate out the remote viewing information from the 'noise' in your mind.

As a rough rule of thumb, any image that is bright, clear or sharp is almost always noise. Yes, it is very counterintuitive, but it is true. Not everything you see while remote viewing will be related to the object you are trying to view. Often this mental noise in your mind is related to what is going on deeper down in your mind and you need to learn to wade through it and find the actual remote viewing information.

You will find that the signals from your remote viewing session are more likely going to be fuzzy, indistinct and vague. They come across more as partly remembered memories that tickle at the back of your mind. With practise you will learn to tell the difference between what has come from remote viewing and what is just mental noise.

Whilst you are remote viewing, if you are doing it whilst deeply relaxed then attempt to sketch, unconsciously, what you are seeing. Alternatively, you can sketch it once you come away from the astral plane, but don't concentrate too much on it whilst you do it - let your subconscious mind guide you.

Write down everything you can about the remote viewing experience including textures, tastes, smells, sounds, colors and so on. The lines and shapes are important too but these other senses can help you home in on the image that you have seen. You typically won't get a fully formed image in your mind of the object you are trying to view, but what you put together from your impressions will be accurate enough and make sense.

If you are doing this using the seated / relaxation method then just take five or ten minutes and when you have finished, write the word 'end' on your piece of paper together with the time you finished the experiment. Do not write anything else on that piece of paper afterwards.

Then open the envelope and see what it is you were trying to perceive. Be honest with yourself and acknowledge your successes but be careful you don't try and stretch what you have drawn to fit the picture, which can distort your results. It's important that you acknowledge both your successes and where you went wrong so that you can improve your skills and get better at remote viewing.

Whilst remote viewing, you need to be ready to try things and even to fail in order to succeed. Follow your intuition, listen to the impressions you receive, don't judge the information you get and just accept it. It may be that the feelings you get don't make sense consciously, but subconsciously they will and this will help you to understand them.

You should also document your remote viewing sessions because it is going to help you to improve your skills. Keep the written records together with the photographs as it will help you to understand how you are progressing, as well as see any patterns in your viewings. Of course, as you improve your remote viewing skills there is nothing to stop you venturing further afield and starting to experiment with viewing objects in someone else's house (with their permission of course) and really develop your skills.

This more complex version of remote viewing is sometimes called a beacon or outbounder experiment. You can attempt to remotely view a location or an object placed in that location. You could use any place that has distinct features as a target. If you prefer you can get a friend to place a sealed envelope in a location for you to view or an object in a location where you can astral travel to.

Whilst you can perform this experiment on your own by travelling on the astral plane you can do it with a second person who helps you to home in on the location. You, the viewer, would use a pen and paper to record what you sense during the experiment.

When performing this experiment, make sure the viewer does not know anything about the location until afterwards. Also make sure that no one in the room (if anyone is) with the viewer has any information about the location either. The viewer needs to be located in a room where it is possible to relax with no distractions around.

In order to remote view a location with someone sending out the signals you need someone, who is the outbounder, to go to a target location. The viewer must know nothing about this location and ideally you don't want it to be too far away – no more than about thirty minutes maximum.

Pick a location that has distinct features, e.g. an amusement park, a children's park, a bakery and so on. The outbounder settles in at the location and concentrates on the viewer and sends them the image they can see. If the outbounder can take a picture of the location from their viewpoint, then that will help with comparing it when discussing the results with the viewer.

At an agreed time, the outbounder settles down and transmits mentally the viewpoint of where they are to the viewer who is in a deeply relaxed state and attempting to pick up on this. The viewer draws an image of the location which is then compared to the photograph of the location. For a set period of time, such as ten minutes, both people concentrate and then the experiment is stopped and the paper from the viewer put to one side until the outbounder returns.

There are a lot of variations on this theme that you can practise either with, or without, people helping you. The more you practise remote viewing, the better you will become at it and the vague images that you were used to seeing will become more clear, though full clarity of vision is not thought to happen.

As you develop your remote viewing skills so you can travel to further locations, peek inside libraries, visit ancient monuments and even move beyond the confines of time and travel back to view events in the distant past.

There is a lot you can do with remote viewing and you will find it good fun and interesting to do. It will be frustrating to start with because the images are going to be very difficult to pick out, but as you get more used to it so you will find the images become clearer and you get more success from your experiments.

Conclusion

Now that you have learned a bit more about astral projection, it's time to put all that you have read to good use. When undertaking this journey, please remember that safety is paramount, and the first step to safety is to think positively from the moment you wake up in the morning.

Remember also that nothing can happen to you on the astral plane unless you let it happen. Fears of possession by astral beings, being harmed by other entities you may encounter, or getting lost on the astral plane can only be realised if you bring them to the fore in the first place.

www.ingramcontent.com/pod-product-compliance
Lightning Source LLC
LaVergne TN
LVHW011949070526
838202LV00054B/4857